SHOWTIME

MEET THE PEOPLE BEHIND THE SCENES

KEVIN SYLVESTER

annick press
toronto + new york + vancouver

© 2013 Kevin Sylvester (text)
Edited by Linda Pruessen
Designed by Sheryl Shapiro

Annick Press Ltd.

We acknowledge the support of the Canada Council for the Arts, the Ontario Arts Council, and the Government of Canada through the Canada Book Fund (CBF) for our publishing activities.

 ONTARIO ARTS COUNCIL
CONSEIL DES ARTS DE L'ONTARIO

Cataloging in Publication

Sylvester, Kevin
    Showtime : meet the people behind the scenes / Kevin Sylvester.

Issued also in electronic format.
ISBN 978-1-55451-487-8 (bound).—ISBN 978-1-55451-486-1 (pbk.)
    1. Performing arts—Vocational guidance—Juvenile literature.
I. Title.

PN1580.S94 2013   j791.023   C2012-905986-2

Distributed in Canada by:
Firefly Books Ltd.
66 Leek Crescent
Richmond Hill, ON L4B 1H1

Published in the U.S.A. by Annick Press (U.S.) Ltd.
Distributed in the U.S.A. by:
Firefly Books (U.S.) Inc.
P.O. Box 1338
Ellicott Station
Buffalo, NY 14205

Printed in China

Visit us at: **www.annickpress.com**
Visit Kevin Sylvester at: **http://kevinarts.blogspot.ca**

Image Credits
Front cover, 25, © Randy Miramontez/Dreamstime.com; **tickets used throughout as on page 1,** © Jamie Cross/Dreamstime.com; **abstract swirling streaks used throughout as on page 1,** © Les Cunliffe/Dreamstime.com; **2, 5 top,** © Levi Walker Photography; **3,** © Leonard X. Oxford; **5 bottom,** © Bradley Mark Rapier; **6–7: legs,** © Pavel Sazonov/Dreamstime.com; **9: dancer,** © Alexander Yakovlev/Bigstock.com; **10, 14,** photo: © Katherin Wermke; **11: Patricia teaching,** photo courtesy of the University of South Florida; **11: piano background,** © Timur Djafarov/Dreamstime.com; **13, Patricia teaching,** photo courtesy of the University of South Florida; **blurry lights used throughout as on page 14,** © Les Cunliffe/Dreamstime.com; **abstract lights used throughout as on page 16,** © Dundanim/Dreamstime.com; **16, 17, 19 top and bottom,** © Robert Paul Weston; **19 right and background,** © Kevin Sylvester; **22, 23,** © Tina Christianson/Ben Pinel; **27,** © Andrew Kazmierski/Dreamstime.com; **29, 30, 34, 35,** © Taro Yoshida; **31,** © Aaron Rutten/Dreamstime.com; **32,** © Franco Bosetti/Dreamstime.com; **33,** © Stokkete/Dreamstime.com; **36,** © John Karastamatis; **37 top,** © Shannon Workman/Dreamstime.com; **37 bottom,** © Kevin Sylvester; **38,** © Stephen Coburn/Dreamstime.com; **39,** photo courtesy Stratford Shakespeare Festival; **40,** © Graham Likeness; **42 top and bottom,** © Kevin Berne, Berkeley Repertory Theatre; **43,** © Cheshire Isaacs, Berkeley Repertory Theatre; **45, spools of threads,** © Arcobaleno/Dreamstime.com; **45, sketch model,** © Sergey Tarasov/Dreamstime.com; **48, 50–51,** Gene Pittman for Walker Art Center, Minneapolis, MN; **49,** © John Christenson; **52,** © Aesthetic Apparatus, used with permission of the Decemberists; **53,** © Aesthetic Apparatus, used with permission of Dan Deacon; **56,** © Al Domanski; **57 background image,** © Yang Yu/Dreamstime.com; **57 inside image,** © Bambi L. Dingman/Dreamstime.com; **59,** © 001001100dt/Dreamstime.com; **61,** © Constantin Opris/Dreamstime.com; **61: Al Domanski with laser,** © Polly Samson; **63, 65 bottom, 67,** photos courtesy Lee Miller; **65 top,** © Rochak Shukla/Dreamstime.com; **69,** © Jorge Gera; **71,** © Aleksandar Andjic/Dreamstime.com; **74, 76, 77, 79, 81, 83, 84,** © Canucks Sports & Entertainment

CONTENTS

To my friends Paul and Roz (and Justin, Amelia, and Casey), who welcome true artists (and mediocre trumpet players) into their home every week. I promise I'll work on my embouchure.

—K.S.

Meet The People Behind The Scenes!

Every day, in living rooms around the globe, kids dance, sing, and act—imitating the stars who are their heroes, and hoping that someday they will be in the spotlight.

The lucky few who make it enter the arena by the stage door … surrounded by screaming fans, paparazzi, and burly bodyguards. After all, the performer is the reason millions of fans are sitting on the edge of their seats, or watching on television.

But there are hundreds of people who have helped make the next few hours—showtime—worth seeing and remembering. If those people don't work just as hard and do their jobs just as well as the performer onstage, the show won't be a success.

This book is about those people, and all the possibilities that exist in the very complex world of show business.

You'll meet a truck driver who counts rock's biggest stars as his personal friends. You'll meet a former doctor who uses her knowledge of the human body to help good singers become true artists. You'll meet people who blow things up, cut things up, and motivate artists so they can dance and sing for an entire two-hour show.

Many took unexpected paths to their jobs, but they all have one thing in common. They love what they do. Maybe you would, too!

Choreographer

Your job? To design dance routines for live theater and big-budget movies, music videos, and television dance shows. Make the moves and the music match perfectly.

If an actor or musician is doing anything more complicated than walking, chances are, a choreographer is involved.

Choreographers need a perfect sense of timing and rhythm. They stitch together seemingly unrelated movements in a way that makes sense. And sometimes they have to do that in bits and pieces that will eventually be edited together by someone else.

Most choreographers are accomplished dancers in their own right. One of the best is Bradley "Shooz" Rapier.

• • • • • • • • • • • • •

Bradley Rapier boasts an amazing resume. He's appeared on shows such as *So You Think You Can Dance, Late Night with Jimmy Fallon, The Ellen DeGeneres Show,* and *Superstars of Dance.* He's been featured in award-winning music videos and Super Bowl halftime shows, and he's an amazing choreographer. Get the picture? The guy is good!

Bradley Rapier

But the achievements he's most proud of are his work on the Broadway musical *Jesus Christ Superstar* and his award-wining show *Groovaloo Freestyle.* The choreographer's work shines through when you see the actors dance and sing, but Bradley says that's just scratching the surface.

The Groovaloos in action

"In a musical, everything is choreographed, even the set changes. The actors have the timing going through their heads the whole time. If not, a bad set change can throw off everything else."

If the actors feel the rhythm in their bodies for the *whole* show—even when sliding a prop into place—it makes them come alive when they sing, dance, and act.

Believe it or not, the choreography even continues after the show ends.

"We can spend hours, and I do mean hours, making sure everything is in place for the curtain call bows alone! We work out the final music, work out who goes in what order—entrances, exits, how long do you bow? Which actors should bow together? When do the lights go up, and when do they go back down?"

With *Superstar*, Bradley was part of a team of choreographers and designers.

Super play!

Andrew Lloyd Webber and Tim Rice wrote *Jesus Christ Superstar* as a music album back in 1970. It became so popular that they decided to put the music onstage.

They mapped out all the moves before even saying a word to the actors. Bradley says the first step (so to speak) is to look at the script.

"There are 'beats' to a story that can be worked out just by looking at the script. What moves do we want to see performed? We work out a strategy—how, logistically, are we going to stage all this? I have to take the vision and make it pass from me through the performers to the audience."

Once Bradley has a kind of "movement map" for the show, he teaches it to the crew and actors.

His next challenge? Organizing practice time.

"It's very expensive to get all the actors, musicians, and stagehands together with the sets, costumes, lights, sound, and the crew members who run those areas. You often work with each group individually in segments before you get to the full rehearsal."

Sometimes Bradley gets them all together only a few days before the doors open to the public. That's when they smooth out the rough spots: transitions from one stage set to the next, costume changes that drag on too long, or musical segments that need to be lengthened, shortened, sped up, or slowed down.

"After a few performances, if we're all working hard, it will all begin to mix perfectly."

RHYTHM TIMING DANCE

StreetScape: Colin Bloudoff, Wayne Headley, Bradley Rapier, Paul Lewis

Always on the move

Bradley does a lot of choreography for live TV and music videos.

"Videos are the best in terms of time. You get a week to work with the dancers on the precise movements. And you're dealing with one song. TV is the opposite extreme, usually very 'fast on your feet.'' I choreographed the season finale of a show called Lincoln Heights*. I worked with five actors and ten dancers. I met them after lunch and was told we had to shoot a big scene that night! I literally had minutes with them all together to work it out. We had to keep making changes while we were filming. That's intense. Actually, it's insane!"*

Bradley has also worked with lots of big music stars on their dance moves.

"The goal is to make them look good. I find their strengths and the movements that work with their bodies; I don't force them to dance the way I dance. Once they start moving, they lose their fear. They take hold of the performance as they begin to feel more comfortable with themselves."

Bradley didn't always want to be a dancer or a choreographer. He grew up in Calgary, Alberta, obsessed with school and sports. Then, at a high school dance, Bradley watched a classmate hit the dance floor.

"His name was Colin Bloudoff, and he started doing these crazy street dance moves. Growing up in Alberta, there was a lot of country music and rock, but there was no hip-hop culture at all. I was blown away. I could feel my own body twitching just watching him. I suddenly knew I wanted to do that."

It turned out Colin was starting a new dance troupe, StreetScape, and was looking

Dance Moves Defined

Locking: The dancer freezes in a certain set position in between the dance footwork.

Popping: The dancer contracts his or her muscles in time with the music. This also includes gliding moves, such as Michael Jackson's famous moonwalk.

Boogaloo: Dancers roll and twist their hips as they dance. This style was made famous by the group the Electric Boogaloos.

Breaking: Features incredibly athletic spinning and jumping, often in time to hip-hop music.

for dancers. Bradley joined right away. He danced part-time while finishing school and then he also danced while attending university.

"I was seeing a whole new world. We were the only Canadian dance group at the time doing popping, boogaloo, and funk routines. We toured across the country. It was amazing."

StreetScape got regular work on television, on award shows, and in live appearances, traveling farther and longer. But eventually—due to family commitments and other pressures—they broke up.

"I was devastated. I felt we still had so much to do. Dance took a backseat. I hung up my shoes. Then I saw an ad for a Canadian talent search. They were looking for dancers, actors, and singers. I decided to give it another shot."

Bradley won the Canadian finals and earned a chance to compete in Los Angeles and New York.

"Suddenly, I was working with and staging ballet dancers, jazz dancers. This was a great education. I was not a studio-trained dancer, but I could pick up different styles fairly quickly."

Bradley won the U.S. finals. The grand prize was sponsorship for a U.S. work permit. He returned to Canada to wait for his paperwork to come through. In Vancouver, he found work choreographing for films, commercials, and live events.

When Bradley got his work permit, he chose to settle in Los Angeles. He taught funk aerobic classes. He danced at parties. He did anything that would keep him moving. Then one day, a chance (and scary!) request kicked everything into place.

"I was a lead dancer for the R&B singer Cheryl Lynn, and she was looking for a new choreographer. With her manager standing right there, she played me her new song. It finished. She looked up at me and said, 'Okay, whaddya got?' I had to come up with something on the spot. It was a huge moment, but all the challenges I'd faced had taught me to let go and trust. It was fun. And I nailed it."

Although Bradley was gaining a reputation as a top dancer and choreographer, he'd never lost his enthusiasm for street dance. He loved the freestyle element of that dance culture.

"I started inviting people from the dance community over to my place for barbecues, just to tell stories, hang out, and hit some moves together. A bunch of us bonded, and I formed a group called the Groovaloos. We just took off."

In the craziness that is show business, Bradley had hit the big time. Opportunities started coming in fast and furious, from dance shows all the way to big Broadway musicals. Still, some things never change.

"I'm always chasing that feeling I had that first time, watching that street dancer at my school. That's what I want every dancer, every member of the audience to feel. I've lost it a few times along the way, but it's that amazing, powerful, and creative spirit behind freestyle and street dance that still drives everything I do."

Dollars and Cents

Doing something you love and getting paid for it isn't easy. Bradley once received a call from a big company, asking him to design a six-minute routine for an upcoming conference. At the time, he was used to total budgets of around $500.

"I was getting up the nerve to ask for maybe $700, but I asked what they usually paid. They said, 'How about $2,500 for your four dancers and $3,000 for you?' I was floored! Let's just say that I started to see the value of being a choreographer."

WANT TO BE A CHOREOGRAPHER?

Love music. Do your feet start twitching whenever you hear a beat? Then move to the beat. Dance is the key. You need to be able to do it yourself before you can teach others.

Study dance. Start early in life—if you can—and study any and all kinds of dance. Be familiar with all the different styles.

Work well under pressure. Not everyone is a natural dancer, but you need to make them look like they are, often in a very short period of time.

Crave exercise. You'll work as hard as any athlete, and you'll ask the performers to do the same. Your feet, legs, arms, and heart will take a beating.

Don't be shy. There's a lot of competition for choreographer jobs, and you'll need to be outgoing, selling yourself and taking any opportunity that comes up.

VocaL Coach

Vocal coaches are the people who help singers hit the right notes at the right time and with the proper technique. No singer goes out onstage, no matter how famous, without a good vocal coach to back them up, train them, prepare them … and even criticize them.

Surprisingly, a lot of the coaching is physical. Bad posture, for example, can put a strain on your vocal cords, causing you to lose your voice. Proper breathing technique is also important. It's the rush of air over the cords that makes the sound. Breathe deeply and exhale calmly, and that sound will be rich and full. Push it—forcing the air over your vocal cords with your neck and chest muscles—and the sound thins, or weakens.

A lot of the vocal coach's work is mental. A singer needs confidence. Some have it naturally, while others need their coaches to nurture it.

And a lot of the job is mysterious. Anyone can sing the words in a beautiful song, but a vocal coach helps the singer understand what the song is about, what the words are saying. You have to help the artist channel the hidden depths of a song. That's hard work, and Patricia

Patricia Caicedo

Caicedo is one of the best at getting singers to do *their* best.

• • • • • • • • • • • • •

Vocal cords are tiny bits of tissue and muscle in the throat. As air passes over them, they vibrate, like strings on a guitar, working with the muscles to form and shape the sound waves.

Patricia Caicedo's job is to transform those sounds into sublime art.

Patricia teaching a master class at the University of South Florida (Jack Rain on piano; Matthew Caine singing)

"Many people in the world have beautiful voices. I think maybe even millions of people have that. But having a beautiful voice is not enough to become a real artist, a singer."

Imagine you're a talented singer, and you walk into Patricia's studio for the first time. You're itching to sing, but she shakes her head. Singing is a long way away. Patricia always starts with vocal exercises, words and tones repeated over and over and over for as much as half an hour.

"A singer has to warm up her voice before singing just in the same way an athlete warms up before practicing a sport. Singers and athletes have a lot in common; we work with our body and our mind, and we basically train muscles—the muscles that are part of the breathing process and also the vocal cords."

Me, me, me, me, me ....

Some of the "words" in Patricia's exercises are merely notes that you'll hold and sustain: "Me, me, me, me" and the like. Other exercises will have you saying things such as "New York" very slowly, pushing from the chest. Or maybe you'll have to say "Unique New York, you need unique New York, unique New York" over and over again to get your mouth and throat limbered up. Try it once or twice if you think it's easy. Then do it for half an hour!

Tight muscles in the body or throat are bad news. Chanting and repeating phrases will help relax the muscles in the chest and throat. Only when Patricia is confident that those muscles are relaxed will she let you begin to practice the actual songs.

"Little by little, I let them start singing: first in the middle range of the voice (which is close to a normal talking voice) and then slowly going up. This process is slow and should be done with no effort in order not to damage any muscle. The process of singing is a process of developing self-awareness of the body, posture, and breathing in order to allow the voice to sound at its maximum and best expression."

Patricia also tells her students they need to take care of their voices when they are not singing. You shouldn't scream, ever, or talk too much. Eat healthy foods and drink lots of water to keep the vocal cords hydrated. And you have to treat your voice carefully. Avoid alcohol, and never smoke.

"I try to never catch a cold or flu. I have to be very disciplined and be careful with the changes in temperature, avoid air conditioning, and try to stay away from people who are ill."

If she or a student does catch cold, the treatment is to get more sleep, stay warm, and drink warm, soothing tea.

Use those lungs!

Vocal coaches want singers to sing from their diaphragms. The diaphragm is a very strong muscle that pushes the air from your lungs to the larynx, and finally out of your mouth. That push makes the vibration that produces sound. When you talk in a relaxed voice, you can feel the air coming from your lungs. When you strain or yell, or try to speak in a high-pitched voice without using your diaphragm, you can feel your neck muscles straining. That can cause injuries.

Never try singing when you are ill—that can cause serious damage. Patricia can back this up with her experience as a singer and teacher … as well as with another line on her impressive resume.

"I went to medical school, obtained my degree, and practiced medicine for a few years. Over the years, I'm more and more aware of how important my medical training is for my activity as a teacher."

Singing was always her first love, so she returned to that quickly, and isn't practicing as a doctor anymore. But being a doctor has given Patricia a deeper knowledge of the body and mind and how they work together.

"Developing self-awareness—a real understanding of one's true voice—allows us to connect with ourselves, our feelings, and, at the end, allows us to communicate emotion, to move the people who hear us."

The mental side of singing is hugely important—having the confidence to believe that you can get up in front of a crowd of people and tell them a story in song. That's not an easy thing to do, especially when being relaxed is so important to the physical side of hitting a clear, strong, consistent note.

"I want to help them be aware that their voice is much more than what they think it is. They have many more resources than

Sing out

Patricia has enjoyed a very successful singing career. She has toured the
world and has released multiple CDs.
She estimates that she has recorded
songs from 18 different countries.

they imagine they have. I would like to help them understand their bodies, minds, and voices and to help them discover that they are all connected. The body and the sound are the reflection of the mind."

Of course, when Patricia does hear a beautiful voice, an artist's voice, she knows there has been a change, a process that has turned a gifted child into a full adult. There's been a transformation. And she knows how much hard work has gone into that.

"For me, it's hard to think of what I do in terms of a job. I mean, of course I work, but I enjoy it so much that I don't consider I'm working. I'm having fun and enjoying all the projects I do."

WANT TO BE A VOCAL COACH?

Learn about the body, and take care of your own. Singing is a physical act that takes a lot of strength and stamina. You don't have to be a doctor, but you need to understand the body, lungs, and vocal cords.

Practice breathing exercises. Even if you don't sing, you need to know how proper breathing feels. Say "New York" slowly, over and over, and try to push the words down into your lungs. Think of your lungs as a big bellows, sucking air in deeply and then pushing it out slowly.

Love language and learn other languages. So much music—and we're not just talking about opera—is based on the rhythms of the song's language. Think of how inventive a good rap song is. Imagine the amazing, rich tradition of world music you can tap into by speaking and understanding another language.

Get ready to move. Patricia has lived in Colombia, New York, and Barcelona. Her teaching takes her to just about every other part of the world.

Take singing lessons. Learn from other teachers and train your own voice as well.

Set Designer/ Model Maker

Part of the magic of watching a show is being transported to another world.

Every detail is planned out—from the giant painted backdrops you might see at a concert to the teacups an actor uses in a play.

A set designer will start out with sketches of what the stage should look like. But it's not easy to make the transition from a two-dimensional drawing to a three-dimensional stage setting. And because sets are so expensive to build, mistakes can be costly.

What's a set designer to do? Build models! These models aren't *just* like the sets; they are incredibly accurate pre-creations of how the sets will actually look.

Building them takes incredible skill and an almost unnatural love of tiny details. And that describes Machiko Weston.

•••••••••••••

The lights snap on, bathing the stage in a bright white glow. The lights illuminate a scene from a living room, complete with luxurious chairs and beautiful paintings

Machiko Weston

in ornate frames. A few elaborately dressed people stand as still as statues next to the carved oak fireplace.

This is a rich person's home, no doubt. But something is wrong.

Machiko Weston leans over for a closer look. Her face fills the entire room, her hair almost knocking over a lamp. She brushes the strand behind her ear and begins to move the furniture.

"The shadows aren't right," she thinks. *"We'll have to make some changes."*

She lifts up the people and puts them in a box next to the stage. Then she flicks off the lights and prepares to tell the rest of the design crew that they have some work to do. That's okay. That's exactly why Machiko makes her model sets.

"The designers give me their drawings or their computer images. My job is to turn those two-dimensional images into a three-dimensional reality. That's the only way to see how everything will really work together, or not."

The models have to be small but accurate. If you only saw a photograph of the set, without some sort of scale to let you know the size, you'd think the photo was taken inside the actual theater.

Get Out Your Calculator

When Machiko talks about making a 1:25 model, she means that it's 25 times smaller than the real thing. Each centimeter on the model represents 25 centimeters on the proposed set.

"The models are exact replicas of the stage, including all the sets, props, and actors. I make everything on a 1:25 scale. That's big enough to get all the details in and small enough that we can carry the model around."

How much detail does Machiko put into the model? As much as possible. The carpeting has the same pattern as the real carpet will have on the stage. The walls are painted the same color. If you look carefully, the legs of the chairs are carved—by hand.

"Those are toothpicks. I use a knife to cut the design into them. The slats in the back are metal pins that I cut to size. There's also a design in the back of the chair. That's another advantage of the 3-D model. You can see through the legs, through the back of the chair as well, to see how the light will behave on a real stage."

When everything works in miniature to Machiko's satisfaction, she sends the models to the set builders.

"I have to make versions of all the props. I even make models of musical instruments if it's a concert or a musical with the band onstage. We also run through the set changes on the model, to make sure those work as well. It would make a great stop-motion animated film!"

Machiko's love of fine detail and models started when she was a little girl

SET DESIGNER/MODEL MAKER

growing up in Kanazawa, on the western coast of Japan.

"I had a dollhouse and I loved to rearrange everything inside. I even used clay to make my own furniture. I also loved those ads in the paper for condos, the ones that had drawings showing the layout. I would play with those, too, picking out which rooms would be mine or my family's. I could see in my mind what that would look like in real life."

Paper Creations

Machiko was asked to make a series of buildings for the touring musical *The Rocky Horror Picture Show*. She made a church (see picture on page 19) and haunted house. They are tiny but incredibly detailed.

"They are made of paper. I cut the lines for the shingles and the slats of the windows with a knife. The roof of the haunted house had to actually come off. I had a little more freedom to be creative with these, too. Then I mailed them to Germany where they made mini-movies with the models. The church starts off sitting on a globe and is spinning around, for example."

Those mini-movies are projected onto a screen behind the actors during the musical.

Not surprisingly, Machiko went on to study architecture.

"That's where the models started. We made models of buildings all the time. There's not much detail in those, but I learned how to make the measurements and build the models quickly."

But somewhere along the way, Machiko's attention shifted. As she continued her studies in England, she was exposed to London's theater scene. She was blown away, especially by the sets.

"I realized that you could take the skills I knew from architecture and use them to build all sorts of amazing things. Some of them were basic structures and others were crazy, abstract ideas. I was amazed. I wanted to do that."

Machiko studied set design at the Wimbledon School of Art in London, England, and hasn't looked back since. She's done models for dozens of stage plays in London and on Broadway. Everything from *Sunday in the Park with George* to *Oklahoma*. And now pop musicians such as Lady Gaga and Katy Perry are catching onto the idea.

"Bands are taking more risks with their stage shows so they are hiring set designers from theater to help them develop a distinctive look. More and more of the design work today is for concerts."

Machiko's models can take anywhere from a few days to weeks to make. And each time a show moves, she has to start over.

"We did the play A Little Night Music *in London and I had models of the sets all made. The play moved to Broadway, and the stage was slightly smaller. So I had to make a new model of the stage to fit the dimensions.*

Machiko clearly loves her work, but there are hazards. Her fingers are often covered in bandages, thanks to paper cuts and nicks from the various knives she uses.

"And I'm always gluing my fingers together. So I use tweezers as much as possible to put the pieces of a model in place."

It's also difficult to deal with the hours and hours of painstaking attention to detail. That takes a lot of concentration. Machiko has to be careful—paper by its very nature is fragile. It's interesting that she uses scalpels and tweezers. She's a little like a surgeon, carefully cutting, pasting, and manipulating.

"People hear about my work and they say, 'You must be the most patient person in the world.' That's true, I guess. But I know there is a definite goal that I'm aiming for. Still, there are days when I don't move from my desk for eight straight hours, and at the end of the day, all I have is a tiny chair and I think, 'This is my life?' But when I see the finished model, I just feel happy."

WANT TO BE A SET DESIGNER?

Learn to work with models. Make paper models, use papier-mâché … and have fun. Some of the best ideas are the craziest.

Look at sets more closely. When you're at a play, concert, or show, or watching TV, take some time to concentrate on the sets. Are the drapes real fabric, or just made to look that way?

Study architecture. Sets, backdrops, chairs … They are all structures. Even if you don't want to design buildings, you are going to need the experience building structures that are stable.

Study math. You need to know the ratios for making a scale model of something huge. The measurements have to be accurate or the final sets won't work.

Long-Haul Trucker

If you've ever gone to a concert or a show, you've seen the huge speaker systems, the lights, laser, sets … and on and on. It takes tons of equipment to put on a show. And every tour hits lots of different cities, often back to back.

That equipment is also expensive, very expensive. So how do the tour organizers get it from city to city in one piece and on time?

They trust a professional like Ben Pinel.

••••••••••••••

BEEP
BEEP

Ben Pinel

Ben Pinel curses under his breath as he backs up his giant semitrailer into the loading dock of the Boston Garden. It's an older arena, and it definitely wasn't built with the modern rock tour—with its huge contingent of trucks and trailers—in mind.

BEEP
BEEP
BEEP
BEEP

The loading bays are tiny, and the driveway leading to them is winding and narrow.

"It's one of the hardest parts of my job, getting those huge trucks into place so the set-up crew can grab the equipment and do their jobs."

Ben isn't just behind the wheel. He's what's known as the "lead driver"—kind of the foreman for the whole transportation side of the tour. On the day of the concert, it's his job to make sure all the trucks go in the right order to get unpacked quickly.

"If that doesn't happen on schedule, it has a domino effect for the rest of the setup. There are no excuses for not getting things done. Each day of a concert costs millions of dollars. Backing up may be really tough at some arenas, but too bad."

Today Ben is setting up for the Trans-Siberian Orchestra, an act that uses a lot of lasers and special effects in their shows. He's frustrated with how hard it is to get the trucks unloaded, but he's getting it done. Still, he has more than 20 trucks to back up, unload, and then park.

"It's a lot to keep track of. The really big tours, like U2, for example, can use more than a hundred trucks. There are only a handful of drivers who excel at driving and are also good enough to be trusted with handling all the organization involved."

How many? Ben figures there may be only two dozen in the whole world. He's one of them.

Ben finally gets the truck in place and the crew begins to unload the boxes and rigging. In a flash, it seems, Ben drives away, carefully but quickly. He parks the truck, and then spies the rows and rows of other trucks.

"I get a lot of exercise walking from truck to truck, double-checking and triple-checking that they are in the right order."

The Trans-Siberian Orchestra will put on two concerts today, a matinee at around two and then the evening concert. Ben still marvels over what he and the crew can do in so short a time.

"That rigging will hold more than 140,000 pounds of equipment. That's mind-boggling, how fast it goes up and then comes down after the concert. I tell people the best part of the show is what you don't see … the incredible precision of the workers who set all this up every day. Wow!"

Magic!

Ben also acts as lead driver for magician David Copperfield, who is known for his elaborate stage act. Copperfield uses about four trucks to move his equipment around.

"One perk of the Copperfield tour is that he usually sticks to the southwestern U.S. during the winter!"

Teamwork

Watching a crew setting up for a concert resembles watching a hive of bees making honey. People climb ladders, yell instructions at each other, and use ropes and pulleys to haul giant sections of lights and lasers up to the rafters.

The catchall term for those workers is "roadies," but there are actually many different jobs.

The riggers do the hanging of the huge assemblies of lights, lasers, cameras, and so on. They are often suspended from the rafters, hooking up support cables and making sure nothing is going to come crashing down on the audience—or band—during the show. It can be a dangerous job, and it can take years to get enough experience to make it onto a big tour.

There are other riggers who build the scaffolding that supports the stages, speakers, and so on. Carpenters assemble the pieces of the set before the show and disassemble them after. Stagehands do everything from moving boxes to unpacking and packing up the trucks.

After the trucks are unloaded and parked, Ben sticks around to make sure everything is okay with the crew, and with the people who run the arena. As lead driver, he's the go-between if there are any issues with drivers goofing around (happens sometimes) or if a truck has banged into a loading dock support (almost never happens, but it's really bad if it does).

Today there's nothing to worry about so Ben heads off to get some sleep. Well, he doesn't really head off. His truck is equipped with everything he needs to live on the road: TV, video games, microwave, fridge, and bed. Well, almost everything! There are no toilets in these trucks, so Ben has to scout one out for his bathroom breaks.

"When I describe my life to kids, I say, 'When you're in school, I'm sleeping. When you're sleeping, I'm going to work.' It's a bit turned around from normal."

Once the concert ends, Ben will be back at the arena to help reload the trucks. Then he and the other drivers will spend the night on the road, driving hours and hours to get the equipment to the next city for the next concert. He hasn't seen his wife and kids in weeks and won't see them for a few weeks more.

There are a lot of sacrifices, but Ben knows how lucky he is to have this job.

"I was, let's say, a bit of a wild kid. But when I turned 18 or so, I realized I didn't want to be a goof anymore. I wanted to do something with myself. I wanted to have a family and to be able to support them, so I looked for a job doing something I liked. I liked trucks, so I gave driving rigs a try."

Ben worked hard to earn his license and to keep his reputation spotless. He started working for trucking companies and doing trips across town and across North America. He constantly challenged himself to deliver on time, safely, and with respect for his cargo and his employers.

"It's like any job or profession. If you have a

drive to succeed, to better yourself, then you will progress and rise to the top. I started looking into entertainment driving because that, quite frankly, is the elite level of my profession."

Part of the reason for that elite status is the huge amount of money at stake in the concert business. Tour trucks have to arrive on time and with their cargo intact. Even if it starts snowing.

"Tour organizers can't worry about weather forecasts when they put a tour together, otherwise we wouldn't have concerts in Canada for six months every year. So if it's bad weather, it's too bad for the drivers. That's another reason why they only want the best. We have to get to the next city."

Tour organizers aren't going to risk the success of a tour on drivers with poor records, or who might quit during a tour because of the stress or hard work. That could cost millions.

"And as a result, the money is the best. Bands will pay for the best, and entertainment drivers are the best there are."

WANT TO BE A LONG-HAUL ENTERTAINMENT TRUCK DRIVER?

Be willing to make sacrifices. Ben doesn't see his family for months at a time and has to live and work on the road.

Stay out of trouble. It is very hard to rise to the top of any profession, but no tour organizer is going to trust millions of dollars' of equipment to someone who's had a run-in with the police.

Go to driver's school. You need a special license to drive a truck or heavy equipment. Getting that license takes discipline, hard work, and years of practice.

Be organized. You don't just drive, you also coordinate loading, unloading, and so much more.

Get along with people. There is a lot of stress and no time to waste getting angry or arguing with people. Get the job done and deal with any arguments or harsh words later.

Instrument Maker

Musicians fall in love with their favorite instruments. Blues legend B.B. King even named his guitar Lucille and wrote a song about her!

It takes a life of dedication to turn a block of wood and some metal wire into a work of art—and that's just what an instrument can be. No two pieces of wood are exactly the same. Make one wrong cut with a saw, and the whole thing could be ruined.

It's a labor of love, fueled by the relentless pursuit of perfection. A person who makes stringed musical instruments is technically called a luthier.

Hiro Miura took his first steps down this path as a young boy growing up in Japan, where he fell in love with guitars. Now he spends his time making great bass guitars in his new home, California.

• • • • • • • • • • • • • •

Hiro Miura sits on a bench in his workshop. He turns a block of wood in his hands, looking closely at the grain and the surface. He smiles.

The wood is ready.

Hiro begins to carve, sending small shavings onto the shop floor.

Hiro is making a brand-new Xotic bass. Xotic is the company he founded after moving to the United States in his twenties.

Hiro Miura

"I prefer Honduran mahogany. It is a hard and tight wood. It's an exotic wood, and I'm kind of an exotic guy, being from Japan originally, so that's why I call my instruments Xotic."

The harder the wood, Hiro explains, the more sturdy the instrument and the better the sound. But you can't just take a block of wood and start carving right away. The wood is rough cut and then dried for months so that it won't warp.

"Los Angeles is the perfect place for making wood instruments. The humidity is low, so the wood keeps its shape."

Hiro's workshop is an amazing place. It's packed with saws, sanders, grinders, soldering irons, chisels, and other tools. Rows of plastic drawers house the screws, dowels, and electronics that he will install once the wood is carved. Wooden guitars, basses, and violins in various stages of completion hang from hooks on the walls.

There are many stages to building a good instrument, and Hiro is known for his craftsmanship and his care.

"After assembling the wooden materials, I will leave them for at least one day for the adhesive to set. Then there's the painting, the cleaning. After that, I add the electric parts to the body cavity. Then I add the pick guard and assemble the frets on the neck. Finally, I add the strings. I do bits of each every day, so every day is different."

Parts of a bass

Electric guitars use "pickups" to translate the sound from the strings into electric signals. A cord takes those signals to an amplifier, which enhances the volume.

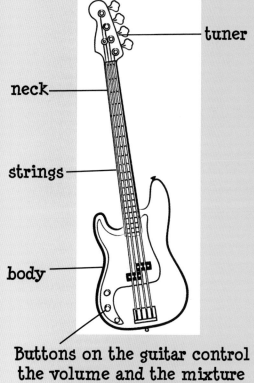

tuner

neck

strings

body

Buttons on the guitar control the volume and the mixture of treble and bass.

A bass can take months to make, so it's no surprise that musicians pay thousands of dollars for an Xotic instrument. Hiro only makes about 50 guitars a year, but his website is still full of comments from musicians who have fallen in love with them.

The science of sound

Sound is formed by moving the air. Your ear picks up the vibrations and turns them to sounds in your head.

Low sounds, such as those made by a bass, actually send out fewer vibrations per second than a higher-pitched instrument, such as a flute.

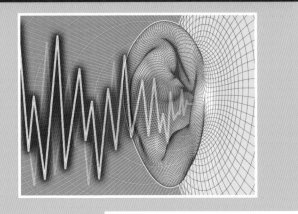

Hiro calls his guitars his children. He believes a guitar that's not played by a musician is "miserable."

"I play each instrument at each step of the process. It's how I start and finish each day, seeing how the sound has changed as I work on the piece. If it is getting closer to the sound I expected, I am pleased."

And Hiro's not just looking for a pretty sound. He has high technical standards to meet. Many of his customers work as recording session experts, where a consistent and clear sound is important.

"The volume and tone of each string has to be balanced. No matter what note I play, it has to come through with the same power. For an electric bass, the low B sound is the key to the whole instrument. Each bass I make must play that note perfectly and the other notes must match it."

Growing up in Japan, Hiro liked music but wasn't a particularly musical kid. (He says he's still not a good musician.) Then he got a job selling guitars, and fell in love.

"I became intrigued by the work of the guitar makers. I watched them do amazing things. I knew that someday, I would want to make my own."

Hiro began buying and selling vintage instruments from the 1950s and 1960s. He learned what made a guitar truly great, and how the instruments had changed over time. The search for new guitars to buy and sell led him places he didn't expect.

"I found myself going to the United States to find the best instruments. I fell in love with the country. I love the way Americans take charge. In Japan, many of the parts come from factories and are assembled into guitars, but in the U.S., instrument makers pride themselves on making the instruments from scratch. An American will build his own house even if he's not a carpenter. That's unheard of in Japan."

Hiro was drawn to that can-do attitude. He quit his job and moved to the U.S., where he eventually opened his own guitar shop. He was done selling for other people. Now he wanted to make his own guitars and sell those. He jumped right in and started carving and cutting. Like many artists starting out, Hiro's first attempts weren't always the best. He still remembers his first sale.

"It was a custom guitar, sort of based on the famous Stratocaster type. It was rather rough, but it was sturdy. The musician who bought it is still using that guitar. That makes me happy."

As Hiro continued to work, he gained confidence. He focused on bass guitars. His skill grew and so did his sales. Hiro believes that each instrument maker has a distinctive style. As a result, there's something that makes a Hiro Xotic bass his alone.

"No two people will make the same instrument, and that's the way it should be. I always make my bass guitar bodies a little bigger than others because I like the stronger, deep sound that allows."

Hiro says he has no option but to aim for perfection. He demands it from himself, and the people who play an Xotic demand it as well. He needs to be, in his words, a samurai of sound.

"A musician is like a warrior looking for the perfect weapon, a weapon perfectly suited for his or her hands, his or her sound. My basses must meet those expectations, become one with the musician."

WANT TO BE AN INSTRUMENT MAKER?

Take shop class. You need to know how to use a lot of different tools and heavy machines. You want to cut and shape the wood, not your fingers.

Study well-made instruments. What woods do they use? What's the difference between beginner-level instruments and really good, elite-level ones?

Train your ears. Visit shops that sell instruments and ask to hear different instruments. Close your eyes and compare the sound. You need to hear when an instrument sounds right; you can't tell by looking at it.

Be patient. It takes a long time to learn this trade and to make a usable instrument. Many instrument makers apprentice under a master for years, doing small jobs and then working their way up to making their own instruments. You'll also make mistakes, so learn from them … Don't quit.

CriTic

A new movie has just come out, and you're not sure you want to spend money on a ticket. Is it any good? To find out, you might turn to the entertainment section of the newspaper or look up an expert's review on the Internet.

A four-star rating can turn a small work into a huge hit.

Same thing for a new album, show, or play.

Almost anyone can offer an opinion (especially online), but a true critic has trained for a long time—and never stops training—to offer intelligent and useful commentary and analysis.

Lynn Slotkin is a true critic.

•••••••••••••

Lynn was 12 years old when her life changed forever. She remembers every detail. It was Saturday. It was November. It was cold and she and her mom had taken the long drive from the suburbs to the hustle and bustle of downtown. They were wearing galoshes. And they were on their way to see the musical *Oliver*.

"I even remember that our seats were in section GG, on the aisle. That's how profound the experience was. I didn't even know what theater was before I walked into that show."

Lynn sat transfixed, watching as the actors sang "Food, Glorious Food" and other songs that would make the play an

Lynn Slotkin

Critics in history

Critics have been around for as long as art. Greek philosophers such as Plato and Aristotle critiqued plays they saw in ancient Athens. Movies have only been around for 120 years or so, but reviews were there from the start. Maxim Gorky—one of the most famous writers of his day—saw the Lumière brothers' early films in 1896 and said he didn't like the "lifeless smiles" and lack of color. Ouch.

Today, reviewers will rate a movie with a star, a thumbs-up or -down, or even rotten fruit.

enormous hit both onstage and on the big screen. The experience was so dramatic, so exhilarating, that as soon as the final curtain fell, Lynn fell as well—into a deep, black mood.

"I went home and turned off all the lights. I just lay there on the floor for an hour. I so wanted that euphoria back, that sense of wonder. Finally, it occurred to me ... I could do this again! I got up and immediately started checking the entertainment section. I went to every Saturday matinee that I could."

Theater had called and Lynn would answer. She started saving money for more trips. When she got older, she worked as many jobs as she could to pay for tickets.

At university, Lynn took the first step on the road to becoming more than just a fan: she enrolled in a course called History, Theory, and Criticism of the Theater.

"One assignment told us to examine and critique a character in a play. I chose Amanda Wingfield from The Glass Menagerie *by Tennessee Williams. It's a complicated play, but the words just poured out of me. It was a revelation. I knew this woman as if she were flesh and blood."*

Lynn had found her voice. She started working for the university newspaper, writing reviews of plays all over the city. The more she studied, the more she learned. She began to appreciate the nuances of all the elements of staging a great play— writing, acting, directing, technical.

"I have a respectful approach to theater. I always start with constructive thoughts.

"ENORMOUS HIT"

"DRAMATIC AND
EXHILARATING"

"A FASCINATING PLAY"

What worked about the play? Then I move on to what didn't work, or perhaps what I thought missed the play's own stated goal. Was it supposed to be fun or make a serious point? I want to let people know what a play is trying to say, and how well it achieves that."

Lynn began to make friends in the theater community who respected her opinion and sometimes asked for advice. They would exchange letters. Actors would pass them from hand to hand, sharing Lynn's thoughts. This collection of Lynn's writing became known as the *Slotkin Letters*, a kind of impromptu pamphlet of theater criticism.

Lynn online

You can check out a selection of Lynn's reviews on her website: slotkinletter.com

"The actress Cherry Jones asked me if she should accept a part. I knew the play, and I wrote her a letter examining what the play was about, how it worked, and why she should take the part. She showed the letter to Alex Cohen—kind of the dean of Broadway producers—who said he was blown away by my analysis. I couldn't believe it! I was so flattered."

Cohen gave Lynn some advice. Start charging theater fans for the letters. (She had been sharing her thoughts for free!) Lynn wasn't sure. Going professional also meant she would need to be more disciplined, writing to deadline, mailing out the letters, collecting money. But she took the plunge and started writing a monthly newsletter of reviews and her thoughts on theater.

"I still don't charge those original 40 or so friends, but now there are many, many paying customers. I've added graphics. I've even gone digital now, and you can find some of the letters on my blog."

As Lynn's work expanded to radio, advertisers began to quote her on posters and newspaper ads for plays she'd reviewed. Lynn says that's an honor … most of the time.

"Of course, sometimes they'll do very tricky things. I'll say something like a play was a 'fantastic failure' and then I'll see the word FANTASTIC in big letters next to my name.

I just laugh. Sometimes, as a kind of game, I'll even use words like that in a bad review just to see if they'll take the bait."

One side effect of Lynn's growing audience was an increasing amount of pressure to give a good review. Lynn says she had to balance that with her desire to do the play justice.

"I have a responsibility to the audience, and quite frankly to the people behind the play. You have to have a tough skin, and I've lost friends who disagreed with things I've said. But I always operate by the rule that I would never say anything on air I wouldn't say to their face."

The critic is often seen as someone on the sidelines—in the audience but not taking part in the main action of the event. While Lynn says that might be true in some ways, she also has a different way of looking at it.

"Criticism is hugely valuable, if it's done right. And that's not just true for theater, but for music, movies, food as well. Drama, like music and even gourmet food, is really a different and intricate language. I'm an interpreter."

WANT TO BE A CRITIC?

Ask questions. You like a band? Why do you like that band? Write down what the band does, says, or plays that you think is good, and support your reasons.

Study English and love words. You'll need a wide vocabulary to properly express deep emotions and thoughts. Studying other writers will help you learn.

See a lot of shows. If you love theater, see a lot of theater. If concerts or symphonies are your thing, go to as many as you can. Get cheap student tickets or rush seats. You need a lot of experience with different styles and types of plays, music, or movies if you are going to be able to critique or rate like a pro.

Start your own blog or newsletter. If you feel you have something interesting to say about your passion—music, theater, comics, films—then don't wait. This is also good practice. The more you write, the better you'll get.

COSTUME
Designer

Costumes are everywhere.

Modern rock stars dress in everything from boots with heels two feet high to shiny hats to dresses made of meat. They didn't make those clothes themselves.

And if you watch a play about a nineteenth-century war or the café life of Paris during the Roaring Twenties, the actors are probably wearing "period dress," clothes that are historically accurate for the time period. They aren't wearing original clothes from the past: those are in museums.

Whether it's a rock star's outfit or a costume for a play, someone has to cut, stitch, sew, and fit those costumes onto people who will be moving around a lot.

Maggi Yule does just that. She heads the costume department for one of the most innovative theaters in the world, Berkeley Repertory Theatre.

• • • • • • • • • • • • •

Maggi Yule squints, concentrating on

Maggi Yule

the piece of fine, almost-invisible thread she has pressed between her fingers. She deftly slips the thread into the eye of a thin needle. "Got it," she says, letting out a breath.

Maggi narrows her eyes again, this time

to help her see exactly where the needle needs to pass through the shiny dress in front of her. She painstakingly stitches a sequin back in place. The dress is featured in the show *American Idiot*, based on the album by the band Green Day. Maggi was part of the team that launched the play at Berkeley Repertory Theatre.

"Sequins are a real pain. Sometimes they fall off. They don't bend, so you have to make sure the seams aren't covered in sequins or else the dress will bulge. You have to make sure there are no sequins in the armpits of the dress. They are kind of sharp! There is a kind of fake sequin fabric available, but nothing catches the light onstage like a real sequin. So it's worth the effort."

Sequins are just one example of the tiny touches that make the difference between an ordinary bit of clothing and a true costume. A costume isn't just something the actor wears—a costume enhances the words and action on the stage, helping to create the imaginary world of the play.

"In a show like American Idiot*, there's also a lot of dancing and moving around so the clothes have to be good-looking and they also have to be sturdy. It's not easy to do both."*

As head of the costume department, Maggi doesn't spend a lot of time sewing anymore. She spends much of her day organizing all the individual workers who make costumes, checking inventory ("Do we have enough nineteenth-century shoes?"), and ordering materials ("We need more crinoline!"). It's been a lifelong love affair.

"When I was about ten years old I decided I wanted to sew. I begged my mother to teach me. I loved it right away, although most of the stuff I made early on was horrible. But I kept at it and just got better and better. I honed my skills over a long time."

Berkeley Repertory Theater's proud history

Berkeley Repertory Theatre is one of the most successful and adventurous theaters in the world. It has put on more than three hundred shows since it opened in 1968.

These shows have been enjoyed by millions of people in Berkeley (California), and many have traveled to other cities, too. Some of them, like *American Idiot*, have played on Broadway or off-Broadway in New York City, where they won important theater awards like the Tony Award or the Obie Award. A few shows have even reached London or Hong Kong.

Who's who in the costume department

The draper makes all the women's costumes.

The tailor does the men's costumes.

The first hand is a kind of all-around assistant. First hands do everything from cutting patterns to sewing garments to adding finishing touches such as buttons and beads.

The wardrobe supervisor handles the costumes once they are completed, cleaning them and making sure they are ready and in good shape for the show.

Growing up, Maggi's other passion was theater. There was something magical about living inside another world, and helping to create that world. She volunteered for every school play she could.

"I always ended up working on shows in junior high and high school. I would always say 'I'll help with the costumes. I can sew.' At first, I didn't think of it terms of being a designer. It was just something that came naturally to me."

Maggi studied theater in college and concentrated on costume design. Despite her years of experience and top grades, it wasn't always easy to find a job after graduation.

"I started off working for friends. I was doing the work at home, cutting out patterns on my living room floor."

Maggi learned quickly about all the tiny details that go into launching a professional play. And she learned on the job how to make a costume that looks good and won't fall to bits. She also learned how to do all that on a budget.

"It can be very expensive for a theater to put on a play about the eighteenth century, because the clothing at that time was very ornate and multilayered. But if we have some in our warehouse we can reuse them."

Maggi says one of her biggest practical challenges is the backstage costume change. Sometimes actors have only a few seconds to get out of one costume and into another.

"It can be noisy, so we put down rugs so the audience can't hear us scrambling around. You might see an actor wearing a button-down shirt, but those are often really cleverly hidden snaps."

Sometimes the costume change happens in front of the audience. Berkeley Repertory Theatre put on a play called *In the Next Room*, which involved a woman undressing for a doctor's appointment. The play was set in the 1880s, with all the bustles and bloomers and flowing skirts you'd expect.

"For authenticity, the actor appeared in full costume, but undressing in real time would have taken too long. Boring for an audience. So we had the actor turn her back to the audience and a maid appeared to undress her. She mimed the movements of undoing buttons and untying the dress, but all she really did was lower a zipper!"

Another play posed a problem for Maggi, in the timing of the costume change and in the type of costume.

"We had one play where a character was covered head to toe in tattoos. But in the next scene he appeared with no tattoos.

There was no time to do makeup. So we ended up designing a tattoo jumpsuit that looked like skin. He was able to take it off and put it back on in a snap."

Many of Berkeley Rep's shows have gone to Broadway and other states and countries. It's a testament to the skill of Maggi and her crew that often the costumes have traveled with the shows.

"I don't make my own clothes anymore. I wish I had the time, but I'm very busy making sure the clothes we put on our actors are top-notch. And you know what? That's a pretty good life."

WANT TO MAKE COSTUMES?

Learn to sew. This is the basic skill that every costume designer needs. If you've never made a skirt, pair of pants, or dress, you can't truly understand how that garment works as a piece of clothing … and that means you'll never know how it should actually fit on a body.

Volunteer. When your school does a play, chip in doing whatever it takes. Help sew costumes, design sets. The more you know about how a whole play is put on, the better you can make a costume that can fit in with the sets, actors, and so on.

Study history. Authenticity is key. There will always be someone in the audience questioning whether the hats are right for the time of the play.

Learn to research. You can't just look on the Internet to see what a nineteenth-century woman wore. You'll need to visit museums. You should also pore over books that show old paintings or photos. The tiny details make a huge difference.

AdverTiser/ Designer

It's no good having a concert if nobody knows it's happening.

Advertising is a *huge* part of show business. Every day in a big city (or even a small one), hundreds of shows are competing for attention. You've probably passed telephone poles that are plastered with many different posters.

So how do you make *your* show or concert stand out from the crowd?

Well, you could hire a real artist to do your posters for you.

And Dan Ibarra and the crew at Aesthetic Apparatus know exactly how to make a poster pop.

●●●●●●●●●●●●

Dan Ibarra carefully peels a sheet of paper off a large, humming, metal machine. The paper is covered with a huge picture of a pair of huge eyeglasses, covered in huge amounts of sweat. The name of the singer—Dan Deacon—and

Dan Ibarra

the dates for an upcoming concert glisten. The ink is still fresh.

Dan Ibarra smiles. It's a perfect concert poster. Now all he has to do is print 200 more.

"I love printmaking. I love the smell, the mess. So much of my work as a graphic designer is clean computer work. So when we make concert posters, we do them by hand in our print shop."

Graphic and gritty

Almost all graphic design is now done on computers. But Dan loves the old-fashioned look and feel of screen printing. Screen printing involves making a template, or plate, with holes where you want the ink to bleed through. Then the ink is pressed through the screen and onto the paper.

Dan used to hand print all the posters, but a few years ago, he invested in a mechanical press.

"Basically, I got carpal tunnel syndrome. When you hand print, you have to press the ink onto the paper with a rubber squeegee. And you have to do that for each color, so if I was doing 200 posters, I was actually printing 600 times. I still hand mix the inks and line up the plates."

Dan is one part of the creative studio Aesthetic Apparatus. He and his partner, Michael Byzewski, have been creating concert posters for years.

Dan had always loved drawing, and he studied commercial art in college. But Dan also loved music. He played drums, and once he got to college, he formed a band. This was in the mid-1990s. There was no social media, no Twitter, no Tumblr, no Facebook, so he made posters to advertise his shows.

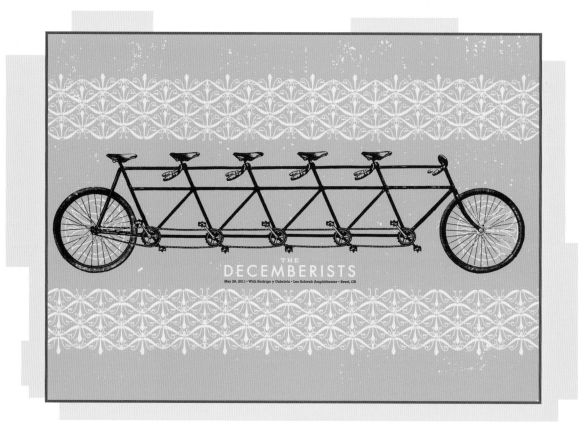

THE
DECEMBERISTS
May 29, 2011 • With Rodrigo y Gabriela • Les Schwab Amphitheater • Bend, OR

"Those first posters were really rough. I did a collage once, a picture of a cog with arms and legs pasted on. It was fun but very amateur."

Dan graduated from school and got a job at a design firm, where he met Michael. Michael wasn't just a talented graphic designer. Like Dan, he was also a music fan. They found they even liked the same bands. They hit it off immediately.

"We used to go to concerts all the time. But we noticed the crowds weren't as big as the bands deserved. Basically, unless you saw an ad in the paper, you didn't really know who was coming into town."

That's when they had their brilliant idea. They knew how to make great visual images and knew how to print them. Maybe they could help. One of the first musicians they approached was Ed Hamell.

"We really liked him, but he was booked into this horrible club. We told him that if he came back to a bigger, better venue, we'd do him a poster. He did and we did, and he sold out the show. We felt really good because we got to see him play and we were helping him be successful."

Dan and Michael developed their own distinctive style—handmade, hand printed, and simple. Then they discovered they could actually make a little money.

"The venues and promoters would come to us and ask us to make the posters. They'd arrange permission from the bands, which was great. To offset costs, we started selling the leftover posters after the shows. We still had our day jobs, but the posters grew by word of mouth, and it just kind of snowballed."

Dan and Michael set up a website. Immediately, more orders came in for their work. They quit the design firm and started Aesthetic Apparatus.

"We keep everything small. We only do posters for bands we like, but that means turning down projects. So we balance our need to make money with keeping creative control. We want to do the types of art we like, and luckily, bands seem to like that look."

Dan and Michael make posters for some of the biggest and most adventurous bands out there—including the Decemberists, the Black Keys, the Constantines, and the New Pornographers. What makes a great poster? Dan says there are really three things to aim for.

"One, it should be beautiful. You want something cool to look at. That leads to number two, which is that it should clearly state the message that this is a concert poster for a specific band. That means a

clear image that fits the music and doesn't overwhelm the information. Finally, it should be well made. The quality of the poster says 'This band is special.'"*

Okay, but how does a designer go about finding that perfect image? The question brings us back to that Dan Deacon poster, the one with the sweaty glasses.

"That was a poster we really worked on a lot. If you go to his concert, you see this kind of doughy guy onstage, dancing like crazy. He gets everyone dancing with him and he gets so sweaty his glasses—and they are big glasses—keep sliding off his face. We saw him once, and he eventually just tore

the sweaty glasses off. That's the image we felt perfectly expressed the experience of a Dan Deacon show—sweaty, nerdy glasses."

If you know Deacon's music, you instantly get the reference. If you don't, the image itself is so striking it draws you in. You want to know more. And to know more, you'll buy a ticket and go see the show. Perfect.

"It's a simple image, but not literal. It's creative. It makes you think, because there's a lot of thought behind it. If I did a poster for the Black Keys with a bunch of black keys, or a Decemberists poster with a December calendar page, it would be boring. The extra effort pays off."

That matching of image and band is key. Dan says he gets lots of amazing ideas for great images, but they won't work for every band. He and Michael did a poster for the Decemberists of a tandem bike with five seats. It reflected the folksy quality of the band's music. It was also the first concert of a tour, so it expressed moving forward.

"You can't do a Decemberists poster with a skull and crossbones, for example. It might be a great image, but it doesn't match the band at all. You don't want people showing up expecting a thrash-metal band and getting a band with banjos, fiddles, and harmonicas. You want to draw the right crowd."

Some of Aesthetic Apparatus's posters have become such an important part of a band's image that the bands are selling them as well, on their websites and at the merchandise table at concerts.

Not that Dan is getting rich. He makes a living.

So would he recommend the life of an artist to his kids?

A sense of humor

Aesthetic Apparatus (AA) is not just Dan and Michael. The company is small but is one of the top design firms in North America and has worked for dozens of bands, magazines, publishers, and other companies.

They also have a sense of humor, referring to themselves as "Minneapolis's best totally unknown design superteam." According to their self-proclaimed, un-official AA bio website, they have "secretly snuck into the hearts and minds of a small, rather silent group of socially awkward music and design nerds. Now, Aesthetic Apparatus is a full-time, full-fledged, insanely unstoppable, and occasionally award-winning design mega-studio. They will break your heart and drink your blood."

Check out their website, if you dare: aestheticapparatus.com

"The question any young artist has to ask is, would I do this for free? That's the only way you'll know if it's something you have to do. Art is something you have to do. But if you do it, you will meet people who share your passion. If you love it, that love will shine through, and you will be recognized for that love."

WANT TO ADVERTISE FOR THE ARTISTS YOU LOVE AND DESIGN THEIR POSTERS?

Draw, draw, draw. Even if you don't draw posters, you need a firm understanding of how images work. Start making posters for anything—lemonade stands, yard sales, concerts. Learn from your mistakes, but don't give up.

Study art like crazy. Art School is a great place to learn techniques such as how to paint, draw, and understand what colors work best. So study! Natural talent can only take you so far. Dan adds that the most important thing about art school, for him, was the connections he made, the friendships he formed with other artists.

Know your stuff. If you want to design concert posters, listen to lots of music. You'll need to find your inspiration from the lyrics and the music. If you want to do show posters, see lots of shows. The image has to reflect what the audience will see and experience. You need to see and experience those things yourself.

Get ready to sacrifice. Very few artists make a full-time living off their art. Many have other jobs that pay the rent.

PyroTechnics ExperT

Modern concerts, stage shows, and theatrical extravaganzas all feature amazing special effects. Lasers, fireworks, explosions—all timed to go off with the music. Seeing stuff blow up inside a stadium or theater is cool, right?

Spectacular? Yes.

Dangerous? Absolutely.

It takes a lot of care and training to properly handle stuff that can kill you, and the audience.

Al Domanski knows that you have to stay cool when things get hot.

••••••••••••

Al Domanski walks into a cavernous concert hall. He's sweating. The hall is in Seoul, South Korea, and the air inside isn't much cooler than the sticky, hot wind that's blowing outside.

Al stops in his tracks as soon as he crosses the threshold and immediately shakes his head.

"No way. No way are we doing pyrotechnics in this place."

Al Domanski

The local organizers are confused. They assure Al the proper permits are in place for tonight's big Roger Waters concert. The show features numerous onstage explosions. Al's job is to make sure those go off safely.

DANGER
RISK

Special effects

Roger Waters was lead singer of the band Pink Floyd, one of the bestselling acts of all time. As a solo artist, he's known for tours with lots of special effects.

Al looks up again at the wood ceiling. Wood … not a great mix with the tools of his particular trade. "No way," he says, and walks out to deliver the bad news to the rest of the crew. The local organizers aren't pleased, but Al can't worry about that.

"These are explosives, and many of them are incredibly powerful. I've seen too many stories of pyro gone wrong to take even the smallest risk."

Al is certified to use the explosives, an achievement that's taken years of training and testing. Not surprising when you know what he's working with: liquid propane, gases, burning gels. Some of these can fire flames high in the air.

This particular tour travels with special, thick metal boxes to contain the explosives, to separate them from anything that might set them off. And those explosives are just about the last thing the crew will set up before the band hits the stage.

"You don't want that stuff near anybody while they are walking around with power

cords, heavy rigging, sound equipment. There are some people out there who think you can prevent an explosion by getting the stuff wet. Um, no. There's still oxygen and fuel in the mixture. All you need is a spark and BOOM."

The results of bad decisions can be horrific. In 2003, the tour manager of the band Great White used pyro during a show at the Station nightclub in Rhode Island. The insulation in the club caught fire, and within minutes, the entire building was engulfed. One hundred people died.

There's no way Al is going to let that happen in Seoul. The tour organizers—his bosses—agree. Instead, the stage will be lit with extra floodlights and low-heat lasers.

Al pitches in on that as well, running the spotlight that follows Waters around the stage during the high-energy concert.

"On tour, you become a bit of an everyman. You chip in on setup, loading, unloading. What counts is getting the job done, and that's a full team effort."

The show goes off without a hitch, and the fans don't seem to miss the pyro too much as they rock and sway to the music. After the concert, they flood out onto the streets, smiling … and alive.

Al began his career with a huge stroke of luck. He'd been working as a waiter in downtown Toronto and knew that wasn't the future he wanted. He had a friend in the music business, and one day they were

Van Halen and the M&M's

Van Halen is known for their "explosive" shows. Not surprisingly, they are also obsessed with safety. They had an interesting way to make sure the local organizers had given them a safe stage on which to perform—M&M's. Yes, the candy.

What Van Halen would do is include a demand for the candy smack in the middle of their safety checklist. They specifically asked that the organizers remove all the brown M&M's from the candy dish.

If they showed up and there were brown M&M's waiting for them, they wouldn't play. The story about the crazy rock stars and their outrageous demands became legendary—but really, it was their way of knowing if the local organizers followed instructions! Clever.

going to a Van Halen concert together. Al said, "I'd love to work doing that stuff." His buddy just nodded, but then called him a few days later.

"Turns out, he needed someone to work the light and music for a gig at a nightclub. Now, I had never touched a computer before, and I showed up and it was all computerized. Talk about learning on the job! I had the owner yelling at me, my friend on the phone talking me through the steps. Yikes!"

Third degree

Bands can suffer serious accidents as well. Metallica front man James Hetfield was burned by exploding pyro at a concert in 1992. He suffered second- and third-degree burns on his left side. It would have been worse but his guitar deflected some of the flames. Incredibly, he was back onstage two weeks later.

Michael Jackson suffered third-degree burns to his head when his hair caught fire during filming for a soft drink ad. He didn't realize it had happened and actually kept dancing for a few seconds before stagehands sprayed him to put out the fire. He required surgery. Jackson later set up a burn center for children with the money he received as compensation for the accident.

Al says it was a little more "rock and roll" back then. He got through it all and got better at computers and lights. The next step was to work with the latest cutting-edge technology: lasers.

"Back then in the '80s, lasers were the size of refrigerators. The transformers alone weighed 800 pounds. Then there were heavy cables, hose, wires. It was a workout. Now they have lasers that are basically the size of a shoebox, and they can do way better effects."

Al started working more and more concerts, at bigger and bigger venues. He learned all sorts of different jobs. He eventually landed a job at a big amusement park that had a concert stage. Al ran lasers, sound, whatever was needed when the big acts came to town.

"Then I started applying for gigs on the road and started going out on big tours. I'd always liked Van Halen so hitting the road with them was cool. I didn't really know a lot about Pink Floyd before I got accepted on their tour, but I became a fan. I'm not awed by the stars because we work together."

Al has gone out with different acts in drastically different musical genres—Taylor Swift and Rascal Flatts, the Tragically Hip—but the challenges are similar.

"Almost every big show has to have the WOW factor, the lasers, the explosions, the

confetti falling from the rafters. It usually takes about a week on a new tour to get used to the show's rhythm and find your groove. Then it's all about keeping your work organized."

Back on *this* tour, the buses have now arrived at the next arena.

The next venue is good old steel and concrete, so the pyro can go ahead. The tour used up its own pyro supplies a few days ago, so now there's a shipment coming in from a local supplier.

That can be dicey as well, because you don't always know what quality controls

are in place. So Al and his crew will run some trials before the show.

"It's not just the big pyro effects that are dangerous. We have different classes of explosives, and G is pretty low: sparklers, stuff like that. But it's still fire, and when you have 400 of those going off in sequence, it can get hot. Once we got some that melted, and left a kind of molten goo all over the stage."

No problems like that tonight. The fireworks explode in time with the music, so synchronized the audience feels it must all be automated. Al says one of the safest ways to fire off the effects is actually to have a live person watching the concert, firing off the pyro manually.

"Sometimes I work as a shooter. Basically, I have my finger on the trigger, and I wait for the right moment in the music to fire off the effects. If the guitar player is too close, I don't fire. Also, if he goes on a longer guitar solo than expected, we can adjust."

Al says you have to have eyes and ears in the back of your head, seeing the whole concert as a kind of road map but being ready for surprises. It's not just for safety or to wow the audience. It's also job security.

"The last thing you want is to have the artist glaring at you because you missed all your cues. You won't last long on a tour doing that."

How long has Al been touring? More than 20 years.

WANT TO BE A PYRO PERSON?

Do well in school. This is technical, sensitive, and expensive equipment, and you need to know how to study and do well on tests. Al says most of the guys today have studied pyrotechnics for years. At the very least, you'll have to study for and pass tests to get certified to use the explosives.

Do well in science especially. Think of all those labs where the teacher has you light stuff on fire or blow up balloons with explosive gases inside. That's good training for working with dangerous materials.

Be careful. Nobody takes chances. These aren't Fourth of July firecrackers. Safety is always first. Even in science class, you wear gloves, goggles, and other safety equipment.

Start small and pay your dues. Concert workers have done almost every job you can think of. Al sometimes works as a set builder. Everyone loads and unloads the trucks. Don't aim to be the laser or pyro guy right away. Be willing to help out with whatever jobs need doing.

SongwriTer

When you hear an amazing song on the radio, do you assume the singer is the person who wrote it?

That's definitely not the case; at least, not all the time. Sometimes that's obvious—does anyone really believe that Kermit the Frog wrote "The Rainbow Connection"? If so, listen up: Paul Williams gets the credit there. But what about Britney Spears? She could have written her own stuff, right? Right, but chances are that Heather Bright was the person behind the songs (even though she's not always credited).

There are lots of reasons for this. Some songwriters are musicians but feel a song might work better for someone else. Or sometimes an artist writes a song that someone else hears and covers, turning it into a hit.

There are also professional songwriters who never perform themselves. They just have a knack for writing great songs.

No genre relies on the songwriter more than country music.

And in that world, Lee Thomas Miller is one of the best. You might be surprised at how he comes up with his ideas.

Lee Thomas Miller

Lee Thomas Miller sits at his desk. His laptop is open, but he's also writing down notes on a pad of yellow lined paper. It's a typical scene in a typical office. Lee also works a pretty typical workday—checking in around 10 a.m., and then heading home in time for dinner.

The big difference is that Lee spends his day with other writers, creating hit country music songs for music publishers.

"It's a collaborative effort. I'll sit across from one of my writing partners, and we'll yell out ideas at each other, working out the story we want to tell in a song."

That's exactly what's happening today. Lee pulls a sheet of scribbled notes out of a file folder on his desk marked "ideas" and calls out his thoughts.

"How about a song about 'the old blue truck'? Everything happens in the truck."

"Sure!"

Lee and his partners start working out a story line together, gaining momentum and energy as the ideas fly around the room.

"We could have him get his first kiss, in the old blue truck."

"He gets dumped, in the old blue truck."

"Drives home from the hospital with his newborn daughter, in his old blue truck."

They'll do this for hours, refining and honing the concept. And occasionally, Lee will grab a guitar to see how easily the words flow when set to a good tune.

"Most country songs have what's called a hook. It's a central theme that the story comes back to, usually at the end of the chorus—like the old blue truck. Each time it's repeated, it takes on a new meaning."

By the end of the day, the team has the basis for a song. Not every idea works out, but Lee estimates they develop four or five songs a month. Once they feel they have a good set of tunes joined with good lyrics, they'll book a studio to record a demo.

Demos aren't cheap. Lee has to be sure he has a good product before he makes the decision to go ahead and record one.

"The session musicians are top-notch, so the songs we come up with sound good when they perform them. But this demo version is only intended for our bosses. They listen to the CD and then decide which songs might work with which artists. But nobody else hears that version of the song."

Sometimes Lee will write a song in the style of, say, Kenny Chesney. It doesn't mean Chesney will choose the song. If he doesn't, the publisher might try to have a similar type of singer perform the song. It depends a bit on what style of singing is hot at any given time.

"There are different kinds of singers. Many can play the role of the person in the song. They can sing a song about heartbreak in a marriage, even if they haven't been married. That's what makes them great artists."

TUNES

LYRICS

HEARTBREAK

INSPIRATION

Tin Pan Alley

Lee and his partners work in what they call "Tin Pan Alley South."

Tin Pan Alley was the name given to the part of New York City where many of the great songwriters worked in the nineteenth and early-twentieth centuries. (It was really West 28th Street between Broadway and Sixth Avenue—if you ever want to pay a visit.) Songwriters worked for publishers, creating hit songs. The songs could be sung by anyone, and much of the money was made selling sheet music.

Songwriters would even change musical styles completely from one song to the next.

The industry changed in the 1950s, when records and radio started making specific performances—like Elvis Presley's version of "Blue Suede Shoes"—more important than the songs themselves.

The nickname "Tin Pan Alley" was coined by a reporter with the New York Herald newspaper. He was passing by the buildings and heard different songs pouring out of all the windows. He said the result sounded like a lot of tin pans clanging together.

Occasionally the words have to be changed, depending on which singer picks up the song.

"There was one singer who really liked a song I wrote. But the main character in the song mentioned his dad. It turned out the singer and his own father had a troubled relationship, and he had vowed never to sing about dads in a song again. So we changed the lyrics."

Lee finds his song ideas anywhere and everywhere. He listens to snippets of conversations, looking for real-life drama and the cadence of everyday speech.

Ideas come to him when he least expects it. There's a great line in his hit song "Impossible" about how even ships that are "unsinkable" can sink. Here's where the inspiration for the line came from:

"I was watching the movie Titanic, and the central idea just struck me. Stuff we are told is impossible, like the Titanic sinking, still happens. I let that sit in my subconscious for a while, and I thought of a whole series of impossible things."

In the same song, Lee writes about attending his grandfather's funeral, and seeing his own father cry for the first time. It's one of the "impossible" things the narrator of the song has to accept.

"Much of what I write is pure fiction, just a good story. But that really happened. That *was the first time I'd seen my father cry. It was true and I wrote it the way I felt it."*

It might seem odd to write something so personal, and then have someone else sing the words.

"It can be hard to write from my personal experience, sometimes. That's a real place inside any person. But I want to be the best at my work, which is writing songs. If I write from my heart, then that authenticity comes through the words, my words, but as performed by a true artist."

Lee has penned numerous hits using this method. A lot of people are surprised that songwriting is so … workmanlike. But Lee says Nashville is a special place.

"In Nashville, we write stories. The singers look for stories that fit their sound, or for songs that have a great idea. Sometimes the song's writer is actually seen as 'too close' to the song to tell the story well. We get a lot of respect for what we do; we're not trained monkeys!"

If Lee has an advantage over other songwriters, it's that he's worked in almost every side of the business. He was in a garage band in high school, and then studied music at college.

He made a point of studying styles of music that were outside of his own comfort zone. He chose classical piano, violin, music theory, and composition.

Country vs. pop

Lee loves all kinds of music, but he says writing a pop song is a different thing altogether.

"Pop songwriters have worked hard to go in the other direction, often choosing deliberately obscure lyrics rather than telling a straightforward story. Also, the singer-songwriter figure is way more important to the pop world."

Lee's hits

Lee has written a number of hits. Country superstar Brad Paisley has recorded "The World," and "I'm Still a Guy," and Trace Adkins had a number-one hit with "You're Gonna Miss This." Three of Lee's songs have been nominated for Grammy Awards. He has also won numerous Country Music Song of the Year awards.

He graduated with a degree and got a job playing fiddle for country legend Tom T. Hall. After doing that for a while, Lee started his own band, a country trio.

"We eventually broke up, but I had written the songs for the trio. One of the top publishers in the industry saw my show and came up to me afterward. He said, 'You can't sing, but you can really write,' and he offered me a job."

Lee hung up his performing shoes for good and began his work helping Nashville's stars tell stories.

"I have no regrets. I'd always loved writing songs, and it's a huge thrill to drive down the road, turn on the radio, and hear your words coming through the speakers. Wow! It's a feeling that's hard to describe. Let's just say it's amazing."

WANT TO BE A SONGWRITER?

Learn to play an instrument. You may not make it as a musician, but you'll need to have experience with how the notes you write are meant to be played. So don't drop band in school.

Study music theory. You might have a great song in your head, but if you don't know how to write down the notes, that's where it will stay. It also helps to play around with music-mixing programs on your computer.

Learn how to tell a good story. Listen to songs you like and analyze them. How does the singer convey the story? What words are powerful? Which ones are weak?

Listen all the time. Lee says many of his ideas grow out of conversations he's overheard, or everyday things he sees on the street.

Carry a notebook. Nothing is worse than thinking up a great idea and then forgetting it by the time you find a pen and paper. Be ready for inspiration!

Promoter

Where would a rock star be without a promoter? Possibly nowhere! A promoter, after all, is the main "backer" of any act. No rock star wants to handle the details of booking halls, working out ads, finding sponsors, hiring technical crews … and so on. Rock stars just want to play.

So a promoter takes care of those details. But they do a lot more, too. Promoters put a lot of money on the line to make sure a concert or tour can happen. They pay the up-front costs—the costs of renting equipment and concert halls, and of paying the crews—and make or lose money based on how many tickets are sold.

Because it is their money, promoters are very careful in choosing which bands or acts they will push. Many pick a specific area and focus on that. Sometimes that means a particular type of music or a specific demographic—an age group or cultural group, for example.

The Cárdenas Marketing Network (CMN) has made North America's Spanish-speaking community its main focus and has found incredible success.

● ● ● ● ● ● ● ● ● ● ● ● ●

If Elena Sotomayor is awake, she's working. Elena is constantly talking to

Elena Sotomayor

everyone from advertisers to venue managers to artists, trying to work out details for concerts and other big events.

"I prefer the personal touch, meeting face to face. But thank goodness for cell phones. The cell phone is never far from my ear. There's no real day off in my line of work. It's always go, go, go. It doesn't matter who the artists are, or how big a name, they won't sell out any concert without the right promotion."

Elena is the vice-president of event marketing and sales at CMN, and one of the things she does is find money. Putting on events is expensive, and part of her job is to make sure that everybody involved comes out ahead.

"The business has changed a lot since I started. Artists used to accept a set fee for, say, a 90-minute concert. Now they realize they can make more money taking a percentage of the box office, or ticket sales, so they'll ask for a fee and a percentage of the whole tour. That means they are taking more of the money, and that makes it more expensive for us to launch a tour."

If an artist is heading out on a national tour, for example, Elena will look for

Branding

"Brand" is a kind of catchall term that's used in marketing.

When people in marketing refer to a "brand," they might mean an artist, a specific product, or a company. A brand can be a symbol, a logo, or anything that lets you tell one product (or singer, or restaurant, etc.) from another. Think of the origin of the word, the *brand* that would be burned onto cattle to tell one rancher's cattle from another's.

sponsorship to help cover the costs. A soft drink company might work perfectly with a rock star, for example. A shoe company might want to sponsor a soccer team when it goes on tour.

"They [the sponsors] pay money to help us organize the tour and cover the huge costs. In return, they get exclusive rights to advertise on posters and other marketing materials. It's not just money. We need to be creative to attract those sponsors, so the other part of my job is to think up new ways of putting on shows or tours. The sponsors like that because it also gives them a chance to rethink their brand."

Elena's wall is decorated with numerous awards for campaigns she has helped put together—including the inaugural *Billboard Magazine* award for best tour. She helped design a mobile, live advertising campaign.

"A good example of this is our Planeta Wrigley tour. We took Wrigley brands, like their gum, and built a nationwide tour around them. We sent out a fleet of semitrailers that converted into stages."

The trucks would pull up at festivals across the country, open up, and musical acts would entertain the crowds. Wrigley gained recognition as a "fun" company and raised more awareness for its products. Audiences didn't have to buy a thing, but might in the future if they liked the shows.

Shakira on tour in Serbia, 2011

Elena and CMN take a particular interest in the Hispanic market. It's a challenge in the jam-packed North American entertainment world, but it's also smart business. Elena says the best advice she can give is to pick an area and get to know it better than anyone. She constantly checks out Spanish-language websites. She sees which Latino artists are doing well on the billboard charts. She even spends Sunday, her so-called day off, doing impromptu market research.

"I'll visit Mexican grocery stores to see what products people are buying. There are my friends at the car wash that I talk to regularly, and I ask them what artist they would like to see, what brands of beer or clothing they would like to see. I'm always listening to see what people in that community are talking about."

If a singer or group she's never heard of is the buzz at the store, she'll go buy all their songs, check out their website, and maybe call them up. Are they represented? Are they considering a tour? If Elena likes what she hears, she may have a new client and a new opportunity to promote Hispanic culture.

For Elena, being a promoter is really about much more than just business. She feels that through her work she's contributing to making Hispanic people feel at home. Elena herself was born in Colombia and then moved to the United States when she was a teenager.

The Cost of a Concert*

Payment to talent:	$300,000
Sound, lights, etc.:	$100,000 to $200,000
Crew:	$50,000 to $100,000
Catering:	$10,000 a night
Marketing:	$20,000 to $50,000
Security:	$5,000
Rental for the arena:	$15,000
Insurance:	$10,000
Total estimated cost: $700,000	

Ticket price: $50 x 15,000 seats = $750,000
Profit (if sold out): $50,000

The profit is shared by the performers and the promoters.

*All numbers are approximate, for the sake of illustration only.

"That's a very common story in the U.S. Yes, it is great here and we love it and we are American. But there is still that appetite for the sounds and foods of home, where we came from."

Elena has never backed down from a challenge. She learned to be strong not long after moving to the Chicago area. She was starting school in a new country and with a new language.

"I could barely speak any English. It was very intimidating."

A friend tried to convince her that she would fit in if she became more involved. She suggested Elena run for student council president.

"I told her, 'No way,' but I showed up for school the next day and there were campaign posters all over the school with my name on them! She had done that. So I decided to do my best. I even had to give a speech in English. I was so nervous, but I did it. And then I won. I was student council president."

Yes, it's a funny story from her childhood, but it's also an important lesson: you can't succeed at anything if you don't try.

"Grab any challenge that comes your way because you never know what experience will be useful. Seize the day to the max and fill in all the blanks in your life."

WANT TO BE A PROMOTER?

Start small. Work on a concert for a garage band. See how many details are involved. Promoters are on the hook if a concert doesn't sell, so don't spend a lot of money right away.

Listen, listen, listen. What's the buzz on the street? On the Internet? Is a musical act huge on blogs, but not getting played on the radio? Do they have a promoter to help them stage a concert? Find out.

Do your research. Find out what kinds of bands or shows do well where you live. What bands sell out the big arena? What bands have trouble filling a coffee shop? Pick an area you like and get to know it better than anyone else.

Learn a language—it might give you a competitive edge. The world is full of acts that are big in their countries but undiscovered here. If you can speak their language and your own, it can give you an advantage in the jam-packed marketplace.

Welcome To The Show!

Finally, it's *showtime*! The big night is here and the fans have started to arrive. Whether the show is at an intimate venue or in a huge arena, a lot of people are working hard to make the show a success.

In this final chapter, we'll take a tour behind the scenes at one of the top venues in the world: Rogers Arena in Vancouver, British Columbia.

Director of Live Entertainment

Your job is to make sure the arena is booked as much as possible, and by bands or acts that will sell lots of tickets. You need to have one eye on the market to know which bands are hot, and the other on the calendar to know when they are in your town. In many ways, you are the gatekeeper, the person who decides who gets in and who doesn't.

Rogers Arena Inside and Out

Vancouver's Rogers Arena is one of the top concert venues in North America. It's also home to the NHL's Vancouver Canucks. Like many modern arenas, the venue serves a lot of purposes.

It can seat 6,000 for a small show or up to 19,000 for a big event like a big rock concert.

Sheena Way

"I have a whole series of questions I'll ask. You have to realize that a big-venue concert can make significant amounts of money. It can also be a risk and lose money. Everyone who approaches me is sure they'll sell out, but that's just not the case."

Sheena says each market is different. Vancouver is a great town for big pop shows, but is not necessarily the strongest hard rock concert market. And it's certainly not the best venue for a band that's just starting out.

At Rogers Arena, Sheena Way schedules the big shows. She's the person who promoters need to talk to if they're looking to get their acts through the doors. But they'd better have done their homework.

"We do a lot of market research, and that goes on year-round. Sometimes we do that to convince bands to come here. Usher's promoter might call and say, 'There's not a big urban music market,' but because I've

WANT TO BE A DIRECTOR OF LIVE ENTERTAINMENT?

Get organized. You will need to know what's going to happen months in the future. A scheduling mistake could cost you hundreds of thousands of dollars.

Work on your people skills. Personal relationships are a huge part of your job. You are going to have to say no to some people. But you might want to say yes to them later, when they are more famous.

Take accounting classes. Work hard at math and take courses that teach you about money. You need to make sure the money you're bringing in is more than the money you are paying out.

done research, I can say that our city loves Usher and they'll sell out."

Sheena rarely says a straight-out no to anyone. Instead, she'll walk the potential client through the process and costs carefully. She'll even help them work out a budget so that they know exactly how many tickets they have to sell.

"I'll sometimes convince them they should be looking for a smaller place—maybe a theater. But I also want them to succeed. The stronger the music scene, the better it is for everyone, so education is a big part of my job. If promoters go bankrupt, that means fewer acts, which means less business."

Leah Foreman

Event Manager

Leah Foreman is the next link in the chain. She is an event manager at Rogers Arena. Her job? To make sure that hundreds of little details are taken care of. Some details are small, like the specifics of printing the tickets. Some are big, like how many people will be needed to work as ushers or what type of stage will be used. Leah is also the main point person for the performers. If they want some weird food or special furniture for their dressing room, she's going to have to find it for them.

Is there going to be a dance floor? Then that's marked down on the seating chart. Will some seats have an obstructed view—a pillar or girder between them and the stage? From the time the show is confirmed, Leah works with the promoter and ticket supplier to set things up.

"One of my big responsibilities is the staffing. How many ushers—we call them hosts—will we need? What permits or insurance do we need for the concert? We ensure that all the necessary staff and resources are in place. Of course, we're very organized and have been doing this for a long time so these are not hard problems."

Leah also has to make sure the band is happy *during* the concert. She helps coordinate their lists of requests—usually submitted well in advance of the actual concert in a document known as a rider.

"Riders list the performers' requests from the stage to the dressing room. Beyoncé will ask that all the furniture in her dressing room be white. That's what makes her comfortable when she has to perform. Rihanna wants the temperature in her dressing room set really high. She's from Barbados so I understand that completely."

Sometimes the problems can be more last-minute.

"We had a band ask for a special spotlight on the day of the concert. We had to set up a platform for it, but we'd already sold tickets for the part of the arena where the platform had to be placed. But my job is to make everyone happy. So we found good seats for the audience members and also got the spotlight set up in time for the show."

The night of the show, Leah and her team are responsible for the staff and guests as well as the artists and their crews. Sometimes that means dealing with unexpected problems. Maybe the equipment didn't make it on time, or a sick singer needs some tea and honey to soothe a sore throat.

"The band Nickleback is from Vancouver. We got a late request once to have a party for their kids the day of a concert. We don't normally throw kids' parties. So I had to find a magician and kid-friendly snacks, and find them fast. Luckily, the magician was also a balloon artist so the party was a big hit."

Leah says you have to be a good juggler to handle everything from placing

WANT TO BE AN EVENT MANAGER?

Get organized. Yes, you've seen this before, but that's because it's very important. There are hundreds of details in this job, and you need to get them right.

Be friendly. Bands are going to come at you with some strange requests. You have to smile and do your best. Part of your job is to keep all sorts of people—each with different expectations—as happy as possible.

Eat different foods. If a band from India is coming into town, you'd better know where to get the best Indian food in the city.

high-tech lasers to hiring balloon artists for the kids of superstar rock musicians.

"I love my job. You have to be incredibly flexible and I get a huge thrill out of dealing with unexpected demands or last-second changes. Flexibility is a big skill, and you need to be calm. This is not the job for you if you can't take stress."

Leah says she didn't set out to be a big-event manager, but she can see a pattern in her career. She honed her skills with a lifelong passion for entertainment.

"My first job after high school was in theater, as a stage manager. I got to tour all over the place with big shows. I also worked at the big Vancouver summer fair, the Pacific National Exhibition, helping to organize the acts there. You never know where your passion will take you."

Almira Chow

Almira deals with the fans before and after events, while Patti looks after the fans and guests during events; she also supervises the front-line staff (security guards, ticket agents, and so on—the people you'll actually see when you're on-site for an event). Almira says her biggest responsibility is to the fans.

Guest Services

So now let's imagine you're a fan. You've gone to the box office (at the arena or online) and bought your ticket for a big show. Maybe you have a wheelchair or a cane. Maybe you can't eat nuts. Who makes sure your needs are met? At Rogers Arena, it's Almira Chow and Patti Matwiv. Almira is the Guest Services Coordinator and Patti is a Guest Services Supervisor.

Patti Matwiv

"My job is to make sure they can find their seats. If there are guests who have disabilities, we make sure they have an escort to take them to their seats. Even before they step inside, we make sure they can access the disabled parking."

Food is a big area of concern. More and more people coming to shows these days have food allergies. They are given special permission to bring their own food into the arena … with a doctor's note, of course.

"In regard to peanut allergies, we hope that guests will alert us ahead of time. We take down their exact seat location and alert housekeeping to clean the area prior to the event."

Audiences of 15,000 people are complicated groups. Fans can't always find their seats. Sometimes they get sick. Patti coordinates the staff the night of the concert.

"We do have illnesses. Our job is to get to the people quickly, cordon off the area to give them privacy, and deal with what they need. We have first aid on hand as well, in case we need to take someone to the hospital or treat them on-site."

Sometimes Patti has to deal with unruly guests. Alcohol is often an issue at big events and can turn an annoyed guest into a belligerent problem. There are police on hand.

One of the lessons Patti constantly

WANT TO WORK WITH THE GUESTS?

Take first-aid classes. You may not need to deal with sick patrons (health professionals are on-site), but you'd better be able to recognize when someone needs help, and jump in if need be.

Study your venue. You need to know the arena like the back of your hand. If someone needs a bathroom, you should be able to direct them there quickly.

Yes, people skills. You and your staff are the only people many of the fans will actually meet. You need to be courteous but also firm. If a fan is getting rowdy, you need to calmly deal with the situation.

reinforces is that the staff members are at the arena to watch the crowd, not the event.

"Peek at the concert. Absorb the music. But don't enjoy the concert as a guest. I tell my crew all the time that if they're watching the act, they're not doing their jobs."

Conversion Crew

Arenas are huge buildings, and they host a lot of different events. Rogers Arena might have a hockey game one night and a concert the next.

The ice surface is exposed for the hockey game, but it needs to be safe and secure another day when there are thousands of fans on top of it.

Shawn Campbell

Welcome to the Vomitorium!

Vomitorium is a great word—and believe it or not, it doesn't mean "a place to throw up"! A vomitorium is a passageway through which fans can leave an arena en masse after an event wraps up. The word refers to the fans being "spat out" of the exits.

Almost every modern stadium has a vomitorium … and if you work in the business, it's still the official word you'll use.

Shawn Campbell heads up the conversion crew—the men and women who convert the arena from a rink into a concert hall and then back again.

"Our biggest goal is to have a guest attend a hockey game one night and a concert the next and wonder, 'How did they do that? Where is the ice?' That's what makes it fun for my guys."

Let's say a hockey game wraps up at 11 p.m., and there's a concert scheduled for the next day. As soon as the crowd starts leaving, Shawn and his crew get to work.

"We start by taking down all the glass, by hand, piece by piece. We put the sections on storage racks that we wheel away. Then

Ice-cold Floor

Why isn't the arena floor freezing during the concert? Shawn says the key is the subfloor.

During concerts, the ice is covered up with a fiberglass floor. That insulates the temperature—like insulation in your house's walls. It keeps the ice cool and the bowl warm. And yes, the ice is still there. We only take it out at the end of the season.

we start taking down the temporary seats. We do that first so the crew for the act can start setting up their stage."

Then comes the biggest and trickiest part of the job: covering the ice surface in order to build a stage and seating area for a concert. Forklift drivers bring materials to the crew and take away the boards and chairs. Shawn has more than 20 crew members helping out and it still takes all night.

"We cover the entire ice surface with a sub-floor to allow the concert to have as much

WANT TO BE A CONVERSION-CREW WORKER?

Work out. There's a lot of heavy lifting involved in moving big sheets of subfloor and insulation quickly and safely. You'd better be in shape.

Learn to clean. You are going to have to clean up pop and other stuff that leaks onto and through the subfloor.

Learn to sleep during the day. Much of your work will happen at night, and you'll need to be awake and alert when you show up on-site.

Check out the websites for your local arenas. There are often small jobs posted for conversion crew workers. These jobs often pop up as the concert seasons hit high gear—summer, for example. Always be on the lookout for opportunities.

floor space as possible. This work usually takes six to eight hours. If the game goes into overtime, we get delayed. Then we have to do the same job in less time. At a distance, it looks like chaos, but it's far from it. Everyone has a task and knows what is expected."

The ice sits quietly under the floor while the fans get noisy above it. Of course, those fans are doing a lot of jumping … and sometimes spilling. Shawn says the subfloor can only protect so much. Taking up the floor after the concert can be like an archaeological dig.

"There are always surprises. If the ice is covered for more than a week, it starts to evaporate if the air gets to it. We have low spots in the ice once we take up the floor. Pop spills seep between the seams in the floor and that causes problems. It can take the technicians about two hours to clean and resurface the ice."

Security Guard

Steve Douglas is one of the dozens of guards who work concerts at Rogers Arena. These men and women check to make sure everyone has proper identification, and no cameras or booze. They may also have to protect the band.

"We get a set list before the show of all the songs. I know if any of the band members are going to leave the stage and do what we call a walk-around. We need to make sure they are safe, so sometimes we are just there to be a kind of wall to keep the crazier fans back."

Steve Douglas

Keeping everyone calm and safe at all times is always the primary objective here. Steve notes that there are several important things you have to do to protect yourself on the job as well.

"I wear earplugs a lot. It's actually part of the rules now, for workplace safety. The worst concerts for noise aren't even the big rock acts. It's more Justin Bieber concerts. Twenty thousand screaming teenage girls can get really loud."

WANT TO BE A SECURITY GUARD?

Work out. You don't need to be huge, but you need to be in shape.

Take work when you get it. Security work is mostly part-time. Steve still has another job working at a hotel.

Take courses in self-defense. Steve says he knows where all of the body's pressure points and nerve endings are. "If I squeeze you, it'll hurt, but won't do any damage."

See you at the show!